Vaidehi Anil Deoskar

7 Decisions 1 Destination

Blue Rose

www.bluerosepublishers.com

First Published in July 2016

By

Blue Rose

info@bluerosepublishers.com

ISBN: 978-93-86126-16-0

Cover Design

Ankit

Distributed by

www.amazon.in
www.flipkart.com
www.ebay.in

Contents

About The Author

My name is Vaidehi Anil Deoskar.

Currently I am pursuing a four year engineering degree and am 19 years old.

This is my first work as a writer. I hope you like it. I wrote this book a year back when I completed my schooling. This book is dedicated to my parents who have genuinely supported me in this decision of mine with full vigour and zeal.

Acknowledgements

Thank you for your blessings, dear parents and lots of love to my sister who gave me the necessary opportunity and guidance for my arduous journey. Without her constant unwavering belief in me I could never have achieved it.

Last but not the least a big thank you to all the readers who are reading this book and thought me worthy of your time

Being this my very first book I am both excited and elated.

I am speechless and will let the book do the rest of talking.

Dedicated to my amiable mother who kept me fit and healthy to write,

7 Decisions 1 Destination

Guys I am a 21st century writer and am 18 years old. So I very well understand the difficulties and the situation of the upcoming youngsters. It also reveals the number of choices one has to make, some being common to all while some being diverse. This book brings all such topics into limelight.

This book is dedicated to all the youngsters who are in the league of achieving something substantial but have got stuck in between. There are 7 days in a week, 7 wonders of the world, 7 colours of rainbow. Have you ever wondered of why not 7 choices or 7 risks or 7 decisions of lives? In reality no one has any time to think through these petite lines of lives. It is an inevitable part of life.

Guys taking risks and taking a decision are 2 different things altogether. I could have very well given the name of the book as the 7 risks than 7 decisions. But I did not do so because risk is a used in a very formal sense. Once you have achieved what you wanted to become, you can say that you took a risk for your goal. But now we are way behind achieving our goals. So I say decision and not risk. You always decide first and then play the gamble of risking for it.

Guys, taking a chance in the race of life is not foolish, it is sometimes a very brave and wise decision. This book may not promise you to achieve your goal but it will definitely encourage you and motivate you towards it and take you one step closer towards the REALISATION of it.

My story is not something extraordinary. It is the story of every budding scientist, every budding engineer, or in general a story of a tyro. You may not find the exact person I have described in this book but resemblance to such a person is for sure. It may be your friend, son, daughter or relative. Read on to find out who it is...

This story is neither a fiction nor a canard. It is a story written from my heart to change the daily or weekly errands into a reality. Please don't forget to read the last part of this book, an important attachment from writer.

I hope you like it. Tschus.

Chapter 1

Starting it with a Bang

"Yes! Yes!! Yes!!! I have done it, finally" said Aloise when she saw her degree as a mechanical engineer. She was jumping out of joy and dancing out of rejuvenation.

That night she seemed to have insomnia, insomnia of superfluous happiness. She kept on staring at the degree, her eyes sparkling. There was a shine in her eyes which clearly showed her excitement and delightedness. She could no longer wait for the dawn, when she had decided to call her relatives (her near and dear ones) and include them in her happiness.

The dawn she had wait for so eagerly came very late but nevertheless she was overwhelmed with good will and enthusiasm. She started to call her relatives, one by one starting from her parents. She had even forgotten to brush her teeth in her excitement, so but obvious the question of bathing doesn't arise.

Her parents picked up.

"Hi my Hon... Good morning its been weeks you haven't called. Is everything okay??" said Mrs Harrisons in her worried tone. To Aloise's amazement her mother said that all in a single breath.

Without any wishing, she just said it all, emptying her satiated stomach, "Mom I have a news, a great one. Do you know i got the first degree of my life? Since yesterday I have officially become a mechanical engineer. I sent you a photo of mine along with the memento of my 4 years of hard work. Moreover I have scored 85% in my final exams of the final year which means a distinction. I have even posted a fine pic of mine on our group on whatsapp. Howszat?"

"You have made my day darling. Today I am a proud mother of a prodigy"

Now that was an exaggeration, thought Aloise. But in heart she felt that she was on cloud nine.

"Congrats a ton dear! It's really a news. I wish to celebrate it with you. But when are you coming back? I would inform your dad when he comes back from work. Please tell me when you are coming dear, or at least give me your tentative dates so that I can make the necessary arrangements to welcome you. "

Aloise thought for a moment and then said, "Mom I will be there in a week or so. I will give you an ultimatum in a day or 2. Is that fine? "

"Could not be better. Good bye Aloise and take care."

With these usual words she hung up. Aloise called up her other relatives and informed them all the news with same enthusiasm. Everyone congratulated her and demanded for a graduation party, which she could not deny.

She now relaxed on the couch of her hostel room thinking about all that had happened in the past 4 years, her first day at the @NIL'SAUTHENTIC INSTITUTE, HYDERABAD (AAI), her friends, the project of her final year and on and on and on. The list was never ending. She recalled her first step in the university. Tomorrow, all this will virtually come to an end. In her final year, she had been placed in two good companies Capigo offering her a package of 3.5 lakhs per year and the other was Mencer which offered her a package of 4.2 lakhs. She was happy but she knew this was not going to be her end. She was not going to end doing a job relying just on her Engineering degree. She knew that a single degree won't do her any good in this competent world. She had to keep on studying and widening her horizon just as her mother. But the question was, what she should do now??

"Should I go for an MBA or should I do MS?" thought Aloise. She had already taken the two important decisions of her life which were successful, though not in her very first attempt. Now this was going to be her third...

She kept staring at the lovely bird chirping at the window of her room...

Her memory went back 7 years ago where she made her first choice and took the first step, the major one....

Chapter 2

Starting as a Tyro

I.] THE FIRST CHANCE

"Shit, I am screwed. I did not expect it to be this bad. I think my luck and the position of all stars is awful. Man, I had worked so damn hard not to get this upshot", said Aloise in a rather irritating tone. She was taken aback as she saw her tenth mark sheet. She had scored merely 83% in her 10th ICSE board, which was actually not bad, but since she had high expectations from the result she was upset. Her parents tried to encourage her but in vain. The following days were dolorous.

Finally with many efforts, "Aloise, its time you make a choice, an important one. You have to leave all that has happened and start afresh."

Aloise was confused. She saw a sincereness of the issue in the eyes of her parents.

"You have given your best shot, if the results didn't come out as expected it is not your fault. The time is never same. You have been good, you will be better and someday I am sure you will become the best. " said her father. His words were promising to Aloise. She was not satisfied by her marks but was happy with the efforts put by her for achieving the success. She had not received any kind of coaching for 10th. She was more focussed on doing it all by herself. So those encouraging words were not in vain.

"But what about the choice that you were talking??"

"You have passed your 10th. Now you have to decide which stream you want to choose, there are 3 of them namely, Science, Arts and Commerce. "It took her parents an hour or so to explain her each of the three choices briefly and its procedure for applying. After they were done, they said," Beta take your time, we are in no hurry. Just make the right decision so that you don't regret later."

Aloise was thinking hard when her phone rang. It was Marie, one of her close friends. She had always appreciated her timing. Marie was a beautiful girl. She had blue eyes, long waist length thick black hair and was about the height of Aloise but a bit slimmer than her. They had met in fifth grade and since then have been very good friends just like sisters. Marie was a magnanimous creature.

"Hi Marie how are you?"

"Am fine. What about you? Which stream would you take? Anything decided? You scored pretty well. Congo."

Same question."Thanks. By the way I am not sure, am still in a dilemma. What about you? I think you have decided, haven't you? "

"Well, kind a yes. I am taking science, because I am neither interested in Social studies, nor in accounts. So the only option that remains for me is taking Science. Moreover Science is an interesting stream. I think it will suit you as well."

"Hmm. I will surely think of it. As a matter of fact even I was a bit inclined towards it. Thanks for your advice."

"Okay bye, I got to go. I think my dad is calling me at the top of his voice. I will talk later. Good day. "

Aloise said bye and once again thanked her for giving an idea. She now had decided to take science as her stream. She had made her first choice, an important one and she was happy. She was going to reveal it to her parents the following morning.

“We are proud of you. You have made your first decision, a fine one. ” She has always appreciated the way her parents have supported her at every step of her life.

She had shared her point of view about the work after her 10th. She was filled with optimism and was seeing the positive side of her approach.

In the mean time she was also planning hard of what to do in her holidays. She wanted to utilise them thoroughly.

She thought of making a visit to her grandparents in Bhopal and put it forth. Her parents accepted the offer and the trio was off to Bhopal. Everyone was merry seeing them, especially her grandmother. Aloise enjoyed thoroughly. She ate *samosas, jelebis* and spent a lot of time with her grandparents and cousins. They stayed there for about a week after which they came back. She brought back with her juicy lemons and lots of sweets which her grandmother had made so lovingly. After coming back Aloise saw that she had gained back 4kilos which she had reduced so honestly. She was 50 before going to Bhopal and now she was 54. She went back to doing *surya namaskars* right from that day. Her parents could not control themselves from grinning...

Chapter 3

Starting as a Tyro

I.] THE SECOND TURNNG POINT .

The sun was shining at its pinnacle. And the dew was well settled on the leaves. It had rained heavily last night. It was placid out there as was her heart. Aloise had got her name enrolled in the nearby college for 11th and 12th. These two years were the turning point of her life. She was going to give JEE after 12th .which was definitely a crucial exam. She knew that because of the famous saying said by most of the well- wishers. She must have heard it a dozen times since the onset of her academic years. As it goes, she had learnt each and every word by heart, and made no mistake in repeating it,

"THESE TWO YEARS CAN EITHER MAKE OR BREAK YOUR FUTURE."

Actually this was copy pasted for 10th as well, the "TROUBLESOME TENTH", she recalls.

A year passed by, just as a Mencer going at 120 km/hr. And then came the 12th, "TURBULENT TWELTH". Wow, that was great; Aloise did not find anything unusual about this twelfth. She was as bovine as a cow. She cleared her twelfth with flying colours, but her JEE was again not as expected.

"Mom I scored 90% in my 12th but my JEE was bad, I could score merely 87 marks, which is bad."Aloise had worked hard, rather very hard to achieve the target of 120. That year the cut-off was merely 105. That made her feel more awful. Scoring in JEE was definitely a herculean task.

Her downfall continued for her further exams. She had sat for VITEEE and BITS, the famous institutions. Her VITEEE rank was good, below 15000, but all seats were filled by the she got her chance. After her VITEEE, she wanted to leave no stone unturned for BITS. She solved a lot papers for her assurance and slogged for hours in her study room. Her parents were watching her ferret out her lost success in her last attempt on BITS. They knew that clearing it was not going to be an easy cake, because the last years cut off for BITS-Pilani was 345(for Mechanical).

Finally the day had arrived. She went inside the examination hall with high hopes. But alas it had turned out to be a complete fiasco. By that time she was sure not to believe in "The God's" helping hands. She had lost her faith in it. She had become like her father who was a bit agnostic.

Her parents could clearly see the disappointment on her face. They knew all about her stars in the space but did not wish to tell her anything. Because she did not believe in it. She always gave a sniff of incredulity whenever she listened about it. Mr Harrison had a bit of interest in astrology, which was also his favourite past time.

"Aloise its okay. The JEE exam day was just not your day. "

"Papa, enough of it. Even when my 10th result was not up to the mark, you said the same thing, didn't you? Every time the same reason is not going to work. First 10th, then JEE and now BITS", said Aloise in a rather irritated way.

Later she realised that she had been harsh.

"Condone me for my bad behaviour, papa. I know I had been harsh.", apologised Aloise for her misconduct.

"Its okay dear, It was just your original you. I am happy that your agitation came out. That was something I was expecting."

"I think you are right. Unnecessarily crying over the spilt milk is no solution to our problems. We must look forward and behold the future in front of us."

"Good, seeing your sanguinity I am very happy. So, what next? Have you planned anything?" Those are the general words of turmoil that give rise to a confusing state of mind. Ever since she had her 10th result, she had repeatedly the same set of questions appearing in her mind over and over again. "Should I take Mechanical, Electrical or Computer Engineering?" recalled Aloise

She was blank. Frankly speaking she said "I don't know what exactly my forte is but am ready to make my next CHOICE". She said bravely "Engineering". Her parents were happy, to hear a fast reply. "Don't worry, you have not scored bad. You will definitely get a good college. "

And she did get one. It was well above her expectations. She was happy but the only problem was that it was in Hyderabad. She had never lived in a hostel before. She took this CHANCE.

Aloise was gregarious by nature and so it did not take her long to make friends and to get into a company. Her close friends were Erika and Arpita. Erika was an Amazon. She was a typical tomboy, she was a gourmet but she was cute. She was taller then Aloise and a cogent speaker. On the other hand Arpita had long hair and she was a connoisseur of clothes. From her appearance one could easily conclude that she was fashionable.

Aloise enjoyed their company. She found them to be descent and not Judas.

"Hi guys, where were you, I have been searching you for long, if we don't reach in time we are sure of bunking the lecture." `

"That is exactly why we were hiding. Lets bunk it once Aloise. Its fun, you are in your senior college and in last year and you have not bunked even a single lecture. Stop being over serious about it. Moreover the next lecture is awfully boring. Come on. " said Erika winking at me.

Arpita nodded in unison. Aloise thought for a while, got convinced and then said alright in high spirits.

That was the first time she had bunked any lecture in the 4 years time. She loved it. They stayed in the Girl's Common Room until the lecture was over. In the next couple of months she got placed in 2 good companies. At last everything was falling in its place.

The last year was definitely the most memorable part of her life. In one word, it was splendid. The days were going really fast. The most unforgettable moments of her life were the irksome last few days in the college. She cannot forget the malicious teachers who were very egoistic and harassed students for their own benefits. Their project group had to literally go every day and wait for 3- 4 hours in the college just to achieve one sign of their teachers. Sometimes they had to go to the college just to hear that the teacher was not going to come that day.

Aloise was an extrovert. She always said to her fellow mates and also at the time of interviews, "I have never seen only the bright side or happy faces of my life. I have experienced hardships and failures sometimes. But that's a part of life. I never wished to have a smooth sailing. Sometimes hailstorms or minor obstructions are useful. But one thing that has never changed is my way of working. I was, am and will be working diligently and meticulously." That was her patented dialogue which was admired by all.

"Guys, I have always enjoyed the college and had a wonderful time with you two. I will forever miss you. Please be in touch with me on whatsapp. "

"Yes indeed. Even I have no regrets about this magnificent and spacious college. Moreover I will always be obliged because this college gave me 2 of my best friends. ", said Arpita smiling.

Erika never liked to bid farewell. She preferred to be quite.

"Guys, I am sure we will have a reunion." said Erika optimistically.

There was a deep silence after which the trio hugged each other and saw each other's faces virtually for the last time. It was a maudlin moment.

Sometimes good things have to depart. Erika, Arpita and Aloise chose their own different path of success and went ahead bearing only one thing in their minds, "only thing that is permanent is change"....

Chapter 4

In The Squalor

"Hooon! Hooon!!"

Came the gorgeous Garibrath express. "How else do I describe the Indian trains." said Aloise sarcastically to the lady besides her who had heard her and was gesticulating at her.

No sooner did the train land on the platform than the platoon of people on the platform fled towards it. The ladies were running as if there was a sale in the train and on every sari there was 75% off. Thinking about it all made Aloise grin. There was a second horn, which meant that the train was about to leave. Aloise hurried to the train and was just in time to catch it. She had made her reservation in sleeper. The moment she entered the train she, for a fraction of second thought that she had come in the general bogie. It was a horrible sight. The people or may be the gang (would sound much better) crowded around the entrance, berths and most horrifying the THE TOILETS.

Getting inside the train itself was an arduous task. Literally the people had made the toilets their propitious berth of journey. They lay mattress and slept leisurely. When asked to move, they showed extreme arrogance. "*Humko jab uthna ho tab hum uthenge. Yahan doosra toilet hai. Tum voh use karo.*".

The story doesn't end here. The worst part of it is yet to come. The TC arrives in the bogie. He was checking the tickets.

"Sir, does reservation has any meaning? Isn't there any meaning of fine for the people who enter sleeper without reservation?" asked Aloise.

"Reservation definitely has some meaning. I don't think reservation nowadays is a pittance. And still there is a fine of 500 for those who do that act." This time there was a firmness in her speech and she was terse.

To be precise enough the TC said to all the non-reservation people," *Dekho, yeh sab log reservation valeh hai, inko pareshaan mat karna.*" That's it and he was gone and the mob was again like usual.

The railway's truly was losing its shine. It is in grave peril.

As she sat on her allotted berth she saw the adjascent fellow eating a *vada pav with that usual mirchi* which she had so damn missed in Hyderabad.......

Chapter 5

Decision Determined

Aloise had already informed her mother about her arrival and so was eagerly waiting to meet them. It was after a year that they would me meeting again. She could smell the air of pune, she knew that she was about to reach the station.

Her parents were already on the announced platform to escort their audacious Aloise home.

“It’s hot in here mom.”

“Hmm”, said Mrs Harrisons.

After reaching home Aloise hugged both of them tight. She had indeed missed them both.

It was breakfast time and Aloise got her much wanted *vada pav with the usual mirchi.* It was another dream come true for her.

“Yummmm. I missed it so much. Thank you.” Aloise grabbed it ate like a gourmand. She relished each and every morsel of it and after finishing it,

“Guys I am gonna do an MBA”, said Aloise aloud

Aloise had made her 4th CHOICE. Her parents said Wow unanimously. ” But are you gonna do MBA from India or abroad.” asked her father

“Abroad”, was her immediate response. So this girl had made her 5th choice. She was fast, and her parents knew that but so fast, was truly a surprise for them.

"I will be giving GRE. Now it is July and the GRE is in every 5 months. I am planning to give it in the next year i.e. in the month of Feb. or March. I will prepare hard. ", added Aloise. By this time Mr and Mrs Harrisons were really amazed at the precise decisions of their daughter. They looked at each other and then at Aloise and heaved a sigh of relief. Aloise in true sense was growing.

"And what about your job?"

"I have decided to join Mencer. My contract is of 2 years. It's in Chakan. I will take the job and work on my GRE simultaneously. I will keep on trying for GRE and once I get a good rank in it, I would go there the very next moment.", it was this answer that both of them had expected. They both were now sure of the fact that their daughter had grown up.

"We are happy with your decision. We had expected the same from you. "

Aloise was continuously in contact with her fast friends of Hyderabad. She told them about her decision and the two were very happy about her looking forward. In addition the two said that they would also consider the opinion. The following 2 days she enjoyed her liberty and the scenic beauty of Pune which she had deeply missed.

Meanwhile she took her favourite novel written by her favourite writer "Chetan Bhagat". She had read his entire series, "The three mistakes of my life", "Five point Someone",... Now it was the time for his "Half Girlfriend." (Books name)She found mixed comments on this. Some said it was good while others said that it is monotonous. But she was going to pass judgement only after she had read it.

She had made many plans for her vacation. One month from now her joining would begin. She wanted to do something substantial during her holidays.....

Chapter 6

Road Unblocked

It is but obvious to get drifted away from our goal. That's a natural human tendency. It is unavoidable and unstoppable. The same thing happened with Aloise. Although she was determined and focused she fell prey to these things. Everyone is worried about something or the other.

1. Peer Pressure.
2. Parental Pressure.
3. Going into Depressions, if happen to be unsuccessful.
4. Being Complacent.
5. Being Overconfident.
6. Competition phobia

Aloise had none of them. She had totally a different fear. Her main worry when she was going to give her JEE exam was her cousin brother. Even he was giving JEE. She wished him luck the day before and wanted him to qualify it. At the same time even her will was the same; she was also desperately aiming for it.

Now comes the main dilemma, main problem.

1. What if I did not make it while he made it?
2. How would I face that situation?
3. If the hard work of my 2 years go in vain then what?
4. Whether I would perform up to my potential?
5. Can I stand up to the expectations of my fellow mates, teachers, parents and all my well-wishers?

These were some questions which were troubling her continuously. Not only her, it puts each and every individual in turmoil.

She had never thought of such compulsions, when she was in her 10th. She thought it to be very normal. She herself was deeply in thoughts so as to what this situation made it so abnormal to her.

One more worry which is supposed to prevail in her mind was her potential.

"Sir, she has a lot of potential in her. It's just that she is not focused. A bit of focus and determination will take her to great heights. ", said her class teacher in 9th STD. She had taught her maths and science. Maths is still Aloise's favourite subject. She always scored good but not very good in mathematics which she was so capable of.

"I promise you mam, Aloise will improve. You will find the change. ", said Mr Harrisons.

Ever since that PTM my father has personified me to be "CASUAL SINGH THAPPA (CST)", recalls Aloise with grin on her face. She liked that title. The name was given in the memory of casual Aloise.

Aloise pulled her strings tight. She had to go a long way and she was aware of the fact. She just needed an opportunity and she had got it. Her potentials were about to reach the peak of Mt. Everest. She was optimistic about it. Aloise started eating Parle-G instead of Oreo and 3 almonds each day.

Coming back to potential, this worry had been tormenting her severely. Everyone around her was being a clairvoyant, making prophecies about her future, envisaging it totally. She was more worried about that. Almost the entire family around her had started celebrating her victory even before the race for it had begun. There is a saying in English which says, "You must never count your chickens before they are hatched." Her relatives had turned deaf ears to it. It was no more titillating her.

"Hi! Guys i have made it. Cleared JEE main. Yipeee! ", tweeted by her as her status on facebook or whatsapp, would have been just an ideal finishing they had expected.

Only it was her parents who were cool and confident about their child. (I repeat confident not over confident.).

Someone expects only on the basis of your past and your present. Predicting the future of someone other than our own selves is the past time of every idle person. The present situation of Aloise only reveals that she is a very hardworking person. She had performed well in her 10th and so people expect her to do the same thing in 12th as well. A coin has 2 sides. So the other side of the story reveals about her past. Her parents are very well educated and work at a good position.

Her mother is

1. An electrical engineer and partly Computer as well. Aloise never understood this combination.

2. She has done her PhD in mobile services.

3. She is an MBA

4. She is got the best professor award.

5. And finally, she is a Principle of a management college.

This list is huge and so are the expectations. The list doesn't end here. "*Picture abhibakihai mere dost.*" Her better half i.e.

Aloise's father is an epitome of hard work. He is also an epitome of struggle. Aloise has always admired her father.

Her father is

1. A mechanical engineer.
2. He got the degree from BITS Pilani.
3. He is a philologist.
4. He works in an MNC.
5. Has currently started his classes for 10th STD students.

Both her parents have been on foreign tours. So the mindset of Aloise is very well justified. But her parents had neither stopped her from following her dreams nor pressurised her for anything.

These are no less than distractions or disturbances. Aloise admits it whole heartedly.

Chapter 7

Exploring New Horizons

"Nothing special. I am just getting bored. I don't know what to do. What about you? ",

Aloise was chatting with Arpita, Erika and Marie. She had created a group on whatsapp named as "Fast Friends".

"Beep! Beep!" It was a coincidence, for the first time ever everyone was online.

"Hi Aloise. After a long time. Smart work of creating this group. I am in Chennai enjoying my vacation. ", it was Arpita.

"Hi everyone .Erika here. I have joined Guitar classes. But was planning for a reunion. You seemed to have spoiled it totally, Arpita. "

"Sorry for that Erika. Bt I am cming back in 2 days. May be v could hv it after that. "

"Splendid. I would also b back by then. Attendin weddin. ", said Marie.

"Gud idea. What do u think Erika? We could go to Imagica. What say? "

"Hmm. Will do Aloise. By the way y r u nt involved in anythin? U used 2 write gud poems .y dnt u follwur passion n continue it. May be 1 day u could publish it. "

"stopjokin" send Aloise with a laughing face.

"I am not jokin. U need 2 b serious about it. U write real good."

Everyone agreed to Erika.

"i did it on a small scale. Makin it big vud b difficult."

"Diff, not impossible. Give it a try atleast. U can seriously do it ", said Marie. She knew Aloise the best.

"Ty guys. Tadaa! I'll think. Got 2 go. Vl catch up later."

With a smily she ended her chat abruptly and went offline. She wanted time to think independently. She sat on her comfortable bed to think comfortably. "What my friends suggested was actually not a very bad idea. I could ponder over of it a bit sincerely. May be not as a career but as my passion or as my past time." Thought Aloise.

"it is easier said than done.", saying is always easy but doing it is 10 times difficult. Aloise was in deep thoughts when her phone rang. It was Marie, she was expecting her call. It was most of the times, she coming to rescue.

"So?", came the voice from the other end.

"So? What I did not understand."

"Dumbo, I am asking your decision of composing."

Aloise was silent and Marie very well knew that silence of hers. She knew what Aloise had been thinking since that time. She knew that it was that girl.

"Come on, stop thinking so hard. Give it a try, its no rocket science. We all will help you. ", said Marie vociferously.

“It’s not the question of helping. It’s something else.”

“I don’t think that something else will matter you more than today’s morning.”

“Ok! I will do it. Thanks once again. You are the best. I had forgotten I have 2 best friends and 1 sister. ”

“Good, and never think about that person again.”

“She had hit the nail on the head. She can literally read my mind”, said Aloise to herself. “By the way what are you doing these days Marie? Honestly I have no clue.”

“Well I am taking a professional course of Fashion Designing. If everything goes right, I will be able to design costumes for the Fashion industry. ”

“Wow! That’s amazing. You are finally on the verge of making it. Congo. I am very happy for you. ”

“Thank you. Okay then All the best for your compositions. I know you will do it. I need to rush. Bye.

“Thanks Marie. You have again solved a very big dilemma. All the best to you too. I will wait for your party invite. ”

Both of them had a great time with each other. They were indeed good companions. The next important thing she did was,

“Guys! I have decided to compose anew. Thanks again”, messaged Aloise on her group. The following evening she found 3 thumps up beneath her post. She made a good start. She could not help remember the proverb “Well begun is half done”. It encouraged her. She knew it contradicted with the Hindi one, “*Anth bhala toh sab bhala.*” but she always used proverbs according to her convenience.

Aloise sat on her chair and removed her composer book which she happened to have abandoned long back. She was happy that she had made her 6th CHOICE meticulously. The choice of a friend. The choice of the company one should keep. The judgement begins here. But even this choice of hers was wrong at the outset, she recalls.

She wanted to change the subject and so she removed the book from the loft. She saw the first two pages of the book and could no more control her memory. It went back despite her repeated efforts to stop it. It went back to 4^{th}grade, a class before she met her true friend. She had fallen prey to that loquacious speaker and those innocent eyes........

Chapter 8

The Awful Mistake

"To err is human and to forgive is divine."

Standing there in limelight condescending talks with her classmates, she was adored by all. Flaunting the corridor, she seemed to have been the magnet of the school. Amidst the whole crowd staring at her, Aloise was no exception.But suddenly the situation seemed to reverse. She was walking towards Aloise without intimation and everyone was staring at her. Aloise could see the cyclone approaching and so was searching the "eye" of it.

"HiI am Sofia. I see you are new to the school. We both are in the same division. So I thought I would introduce myself."

"Oh! I am Aloise. I was in A div. in 3rd std and now I am in B."

Aloise was impressed by Sofia at their first meeting. She had never imagined hcr to turn out into a Kleptomaniac. It was since then that their friendship evolved, and slowly it turned to trustworthy. By the time they were best friends, Sofia was already deeply in love with Aloise's ability to write poems so perspicaciously. She was so mad behind them that she wanted Aloise to give it all to her. Aloise eat first was stunned at her demands. Aloise knew that it was not a big deal so she agreed but was not aware of her cruel intentions. That friendship had made her totally blind.

It was only a month later that the curtains revealed the concealed truth. She could neither believe her eyes nor her ears.

Every year a small competition was held in the school named as BOT, which encouraged the children to showcase their talents. It was only for the primary section. It was watched by all, the entire school. There was no winning or losing. It was benefit of talent (BOT). Your talent was voted out by the judges. Those votes give you name, fame and some gift. The competition was judged by 3 judges who were really unbiased, the Principal, the Vice-Principal and the student committee (Prefects, Head girl, Head boy.). These points indirectly added your chances of getting a kind of further scholarship.

Now, Sofia had participated in it. Till that point there was no problem. She was supposed to showcase "her" talent, but in turn she showed the poems written by Aloise much to Aloise's surprise. She was flabbergasted at her genuine behaviour. She was cleverly fooled by that cunning fox. Sofia had not even hinted Aloise about the competition. That made Aloise further unhappy. Sofia had tried all possible ways to prevent her from seeing that notice on the notice board as well. Sofia won the hearts of many but lost the faith of Aloise. Aloise had made no good friends. Moreover she was of an introvert. She was not as genial as Sofia, so cross questioning Sofia was completely ruled out. No one would have supported her as compared to her counterpart Sofia.

Sofia but obviously, got a huge scholarship worth Rs.5000. Every one praised *"her"* creativity, innovation and *"her"* beautiful calligraphy, which was all supposed to have been Aloise's.

Aloise's heart was broken. Her so called best friend had mulcted her for fame. Her heart was broken. it was shattered to small pieces and had completely last faith in the term of "best friend". From then on she never intended on having one.

It was very early to say that, thought Aloise when she saw Marie. Her div was again changed in 4^{th}STD, now she was in c div. and Sofia was still in B. Marie seemed to be naive to jealousy. She was an ingenuous person and was good in studies but Aloise was cautious. She never took a step forward to close friend. She was trepid. Finally not able to control,

Marie asked her one day, “What’s wrong with you? Why do you behave abnormally when I ask you out for a coffee or a nightout or hangover? Why do you always decline my suggestion of studying together? I am not a lesbian. ”

At first Aloise was shocked. “Just nothing. Let’s go, it’s our maths lecture. May be I would answer it sometime later.” Marie had always liked being straightforward, she never beat around the bush.

“Well its 15 min to 11 and our lecture begins at 11. Moreover no teacher is always on time, they happen to follow the IST, the “Indian Stretchable Time” rather than “Indian Standard Time”. So this much time is more than enough for justifying yourself, if at all you have any.”, her tone was that of an irritated person.

Aloise could not no more contain it to herself and so she told the entire story to Marie. Marie had heard her patiently and felt sorry for her.

“I will never cheat you. It is not in my blood. ” She extended her hand for a handshake and Aloise happily accepted it. She had needed that much awaited drinks break. She had been playing exasperating innings.

There was a lot of difference between the Aloise in 2nd grade and the one who has graduated. Aloise is an extrovert, gregarious, and perspicacious. She has turned into a new leaf. But the only thing that she could not efface from her memory was the bitter friendship that she had made.....

Chapter 9

One Last Lap

Aloise took her pen, and scribbled whatever came to her mind. She herself could not imagine her creativity. It just came out, out from her heart.

Drowning Down.

Amidst these blue waters and the thick canopy of Amazon,
I stand emasculated,
Waiting for first aid from within or from outside.
Praying there alone in the dark
Light, was what I was yearning since dawn.

I feel the God is being punitive,
And is castigating for all possible sins of mine,
No more harangues and eulogizations,
Because I am doomed tonight.

What a captivating sight it was
A lion amiable with a horse.
Just as a client to his boss?
The latter being possible but the former is just so crass.

Still, leaving it all behind,
I still believe in time,
Placating God is difficult
But being optimistic is wise.

We must always think
"Gone are the cocky people,
Gone is the trickster's sway,
Gone are the days of hatred and throes,"
But in reality, "Gone are the days of divine."

The day hatred and aggression will be gone,
The day we will have happiness all around,
That day I think, the whole world might have got a
Luck By Chance.

……..

Aloise was a prolific composer. She composed real well. This was the first song after many years. She felt relieved and satisfied but had developed a hunger for more. She herself was amazed looking at her ability not evaporated even after so long. Soon she had the tenacity of writing poems and short stories.

It was not just these protean poems that she wrote. She even tried her pen at short stories. It was just a week left, after which she would formally enter the world of profession. She was ready with her book of stories and poems which was of about 180 pages. She was proud of it.

"Hi guys! Wassup? I am ready wit my buk of poems n stories. Thanks everyone. It gave me immense pleasure, seriously."

Aloise was online with her 3 friends on whatsapp. She could not wait to tell them about it.

"Wow, i can't wait to c it.", wrote Arpita.

"Gud, is every1 back?", wrote Erika.

A triple yes from the trio made Erika happy, she added, "So reunion plans?? Imagica has got exhorbitant prices."

"I think it should wait. I am busy pursuing my course.", said Marie

"In a vk I have my Mencer."

"I thnk even I am busy. U c i am aspiring to bcme a good guitar player."

Erika, actually wanted to become a virtuoso of Guitar, but she had always kept ot be clandestine. Only Aloise knew that.

"Then I c it vud b better to meet sometym latr. Even I have my joining at mencer.", added Arpita.

"I am sure destiny will help us meet each other, for sure. I think we must wait for the correct time."Erika suggested.

"Hmm, okay then meet u latr. Bye"

"Till then al d bst every1",saidArpita.

The chat was over. Everyone was indeed busy with something or other.

Aloise also had started taking MBA seriously. She took the most popular guide for GRE, the GRE BARRONS. She was resolute towards pursuing a good college in America. 6 weeks from now would be her GRE.....

Chapter 10

The Plan to Risk

Aloise will always remember 2 very important days.

1. When she had gone to the school the first time. Everyone cries at this time. It is obvious. We change our working zones, from home sweet home to a school.
2. When she went to her job for the first time. It is altogether a great experience.

She knew it was not going to be easy. When Aloise had taken up engineer as her career option, she was never aware of her other possible options, because she never had trust in them. But now she was confident about her book.

After her entire day, what she remembers the most is the delicious food and energetic coffee. For her that was the centre of attraction. It fascinated her. Aloise was very fastidious about food.

“How was your first day at work Aloise?”, asked her father. Apparently they were out for dinner, celebrating.

“Good dad. I loved the canteen. I had *poha* for breakfast, a type of *thali* for lunch with a jelibi in dessert and at 4 pm, I got a coffee. The food was luscious.”

Her parents could not control their laughter.

“And the work, of course.”, added Aloise.

"I made many good friends on the very first day. There were many more freshers in my department just like me. I found that 2 or 3 of them were from IIT and IIIT's. I sit just under the fan."

"The food's good."Aloise changed the topic smartly. She was good at that.

"Aloise, how is your GRE preparation going on?"

They had done it again. The effulgence face of Aloise had turned into a red chilly. She had always thought that her parents kept on harrying her on that GRE ever since she had made that decision. She had always got irritated. But the fact was that her parents were not forcing her or worrying her for any reason, they were just making sure that she is aware of her tasks.

It was late at night when they reached home. Aloise was still angry and so went to bed straightaway.

The next morning her father had made up for the night. He was very good at convincing. They had breakfast together and everyone dispersed to their working stations. Today Aloise had decided to do some part of that book, the GRE guide.

Days passed by and the date of her exam came closer and closer. Finally she was ready. She did not have a scintilla of fear for it.Aloise had not been in touch with her friends for months. Her only focus was GRE. She gave her exam properly and was happy. The results were supposed to come 6 weeks later, for which she waited patiently.

In the meanwhile she was going to celebrate the 1 year anniversary of her Mencer job, the day after tomorrow. She was not a wastrel, and was not going to make it look pompous. So she thought of celebrating only with her parents.

Her GRE scores were out. She had scored good. She applied for foreign colleges for MBA. She did not get the topmost MBA college but she grabbed a very good one. The academic sessions was supposed to begin an year later. By that she would have completed her 2 year bonding with Mencer and then would leave that job to do management. Her choice of college was America. So she was going to leave India 3 months before.

She was enjoying her job. Her following days were a bit tedious and the intricacies kept on increasing, but still she loved it. She did not have any complaint or any grudges against anyone of any sort. She was gong through her calendar to find how many days she had been working, when she happen to have a glance at the next month's 15th.

She knew that a month later it was going to be her 25th birthday (quarter of century) and the anniversary of her parents. She had decided what to do. She was going to give a grand return gift to her parents(from her birthday, point of view) which would also be a kind of "*Guru Dakshina*" , and all this she was going to do surreptitiously.

Chapter 11

The Final Destination - 7

She had exactly 1 month to put her plan into reality.

"You sure Marie? I am still a bit confused." Aloise had called Marie. She normally does when she is in turmoil.

"Yes, I think you must start executing it, because if you don't start now, may be you will have to do everything in a very short span of time. Your plan is perfect. I trust your ability and potential."

"But what if it turns out to be a failure?"

"Nothing, isn't failure a stepping stone to success?" Marie was pretending to act like Shah Rukh Khan in DDLJ. Aloise knew that she wanted to say, "Aloise, *Aise badi badi shehron me choti choti batein hoti rehti hai.*" She was a big fan SRK. Her forte is to design a costume for him for one of his movies.

"Are you listening? Hello??"

"Ya. Ya. I am here. But where would we find a publisher? Do you have any one in your contacts?"

"Not exactly. But you can search on Google. "

"Why don't you drop to my house. We could do it together. I hope you don't have any courses now.", Aloise wanted her desperately.

"Good idea. I will be there in 15-20 minutes."

“Right, Bye.”

Marie was rarely late. She landed precisely in 20 minutes.

The door knocked. “Hello Uncle, Hello Aunty. How are you?” she was as jovial as ever.

“Hello beta. We are fine. You are coming after a very long time. Come in. Aloise is waiting for you in her room. You join her and I will get you some snacks soon.”

“Thank you aunty.”

Marie soon ensconced herself in my room and they were discussing. They were so engrossed that they did not know when the snacks came. Finally they found a publisher, an authentic one. They did not want to waste any time, so they immediately took off.

“Mom, I will be back in an hour”, Aloise conveyed to her mother.

The publisher was at half an hour distance from Aloise’s house. They took an appointment and went inside. Luckily he was free. He was huge and looked like a militant. He had eyes which were as sharp as an owl’s, which were shielded by those round oversized spectacles. Aloise wanted to laugh out loud, but she was silent because she was seeking help, an urgent one.

“Hi sir. Myself, Aloise and she is my friend Marie”, Aloise engendered her hand for a handshake which was very elegantly accepted by that man.

“Hi children. I am Mr Ludin. Tell me how can I help you? ”, he gestured the duo to take a seat.

"Sir I am going to be 25 on the coming 15thSeptember. I have written a small book of180 pages."Aloise showed it to him. She added, "I would be obliged if you would publish it for me on 14th September."

Aloise and Marie, both could infer from his expression that he was shocked. Recovering, Mr Ludin said, "Okay, you got to be fooling me. You are still 24 and what on earth makes you think that I would publish such a young beginner?"

"Sir I have come here with lots of hope and not lump of surety. I am sure you would have some issues with my capabilities. Weren't most of the writers of the popular books you published, at some point beginners? Didn't you trust them? Then why not me? Sir I cannot force you, I can just make a request, a simple one. " Marie was impressed and so was Mr Ludin.

Mr Ludin took some time, glanced at the model of the book bought by Aloise and then said,

"Okay I agree to publish your piece of work. Can you brief it?"

"Sir it is a mixture of poems and short stories. The poems are devoted to all my well wishers and my parents who were always with me; it is devoted to them who felt that I was of paramount importance. It also reveals of my hardships and struggle."

"I am impressed at your originality. One last question. Why on 14th and not 15th ?"Aloise had expected it.

"15th is my birthday and also the anniversary of my parents. I wanted this book to be a *guru dakshina* to my parents. If this book is published on 14th and if by God's grace it does not become a flop show, I would give a copy of it to my parents as a memento. I have kept it hiding from them."

By this time Aloise had definitely taken away Mr Ludin's heart. Mr Ludin was completely impressed by the authenticity of Aloise.

"Okay then let's make a deal. The share is 60 40. I get 60% of the profit and you get 40%. Are you okay with it?"

Aloise looked at Marie who was completely OK with it.

"Deal sir. Thank you. Thanks a lot."

"Okay then your book will hit the stores on 14th"

"Yes. Good day sir. It was a pleasure meeting you."

"Same here."

With that our deal was packed and sealed. This was her 7th DECISION which in true ways was an independent one.Aloise, now only waited for the 14th morning.

"Thanks Marie."

This piece of information was only between the two of them, not even Arpita and Erika. It was really a clandestine mission......

Chapter 12

The Showdown at Mumbai

The 14thmorning was taking a very long time, but eventually it arrived.

“Trriing! Trriingg!.......”, ranged Aloise’s mobile. She had preponed her alarm by an hour. It was 6. She was excited, her heart was beating much faster than usual. Her mobile rang. It was an unknown number.

“Good morning Aloise. Mr. Luddin here. Your book is published and one copy is already on its way to your house. You have really done a good piece of work. I have read it atleast for 2 times since it is published. ”

Aloise was surprised. Mr Ludin was really extolling her. “Thank you sir. I would be at the door to receive the copy. ”

Within an hour she heard a knock on her door. She rushed to the door not allowing her mother to open it. Mrs Harrison’s by this time had already smelt a rat. A spider web was weaving in her mind. But she pretended to know nothing.

Aloise half - opened the door, took the parcel and rushed back to her room shutting it behind. On opening it, she saw her beautifully designed book. For a moment she could not believe that she had herself written it. She glanced through the pages and called Marie.

“Marie, my book has hit the stores.---”

Cutting Aloise in between, Marie said, "Wow, Aloise it is awesome. I took a copy of it from the nearest stores. I have finished a quarter of it, and I am totally mesmerised in it. "

"Oh, Thank you. Why don't you come to my house?"

"I am already on my way, dear. Will be there in 5."

"Okay."

Aloise immediately fastened her pace and brushed and combed. She was just ready when the bell rang. This time she did not rush forth, her mother opened the door. Marie greeted everyone and straight away came and hugged Aloise.

"Wow my writer. I am so proud of you."

"Thank you. Even I received a copy of it. I have a brilliant idea."

She turned on her internet. She thought of telling everyone about the book. But,

"Tun tun do.......", rang her mobile. She opened her whatsapp and she already had some unread messages.

"Congo"

"Congo".....

Many messages of this kind she saw.

"Ty every1. Without your encouragement and support it was impossible. Guys tomm is my birthday, plz do come Arpita, Marie and Erika. The dinners on me. Tomm sharp at 6 pm. A virtual get together at my place. No gifts", she replied. She typed her address for no confusion.

Her mobile rang which indicated a call from Mr Ludin. She had saved his number.

"Hallo, budding writer. Your book has hit the entire city and also a part of Mumbai. A million copies are sold, and ever since many calls have been appreciating your creativity."

"Thank you, sir. It would never have been possible without your co-operation and support."

"What next? When would you be ready with the next one?"

The next question astonished Aloise much more. "Well not so early sir."

They both were laughing at their ends. They ended the call.

"Thank you, Marie. You are the real hero."

"Friendship main no sorry and no thank you."

"What do you think about my parent's reaction?"

"Wait and watch. Its gonna be a real surprise. I will be there at 5:30."

Aloise was very happy with her success. It was not huge as that of ChetanBhagat, but she was happy that everybody had liked it and enjoyed reading it. That night Aloise slept tight. She knew the day after was going to be hectic. She would have to give a twin party.

Chapter 13

And a Twin Party

"Happy Birthday Aloise. Wake up birthday girl!!" yelled Mr Harrisons. Aloise woke up instantly. She knew that it was her day.

"Thanks mom, Thanks Dad. Where's my cake? I have been dreaming about it the whole night."

"Brush your teeth and freshen up, before that, lazy bone."

Aloise quickly freshened up and was on the dining table with her return gift well packed. When she reached the table she found that her gift was already well packed on her seat. Her parents got the birthday cake, her favourite one

"Wow, mom, isn't it the Mickey mouse made by you."

Mrs Harrisons smiled and they cut it with the usual song of Happy Birthday To You....... Before Aloise opened her gift, she engendered her hand with the return gift.

"What is this, Aloise?"

"Nothing much mom. Just a special kind of return gift. Thank you for shaping the beautiful 25 years of my life. A very, very happy Anniversary to you both."

"Thank you. But,--"

Aloise hugged her parents and urged them to open it. She could see their anxiety and curiosity while opening it and their scintillating faces when they opened it.

"Wow. What's this? When..........", a lot of question were pouring from their minds.

"Read on parents. I hope you like it. This is purely dedicated to you, by me."

Together they read, read and read. They had finished half the book when they rose and said," Aloise this is really unbelievable. We knew that you loved writing poems but did not know that you do it so adroitly. It is no less than a professional poem."

"Thank you dear. We are so very proud of you. But who published it and when did you speak to that person? "

"The pleasure is all mine. The person who published my book is Mr. Ludin and it was me and Marie who went to talk to him in person. Mom, I have invited 3 of my very close friends for dinner tonight. Are you okay with that?"

"Arpita, Marie and Erika? "

"How did you know that I had invited them?"

"I have already given them a formal invite. I know you very close friends."

"Oh mom, Thank you."

Aloise's mother showed Aloise all the wishes. She was happy seeing them.

"Shall I help you with any preparations? We still have 6 hours before they come. I have asked only Marie to come a bit early at 5:30."

"No problem. You are the birthday girl tonight. You need not assist. Your father has a holiday today, and will provide me assistance, as always. You just give me the menu. "

"Showcase your best. I know you have already got something on your mind. But please don't do any fashion mom. No more fashion disasters. "

Aloise, from the corner of her eye saw her father laughing at the fact she had just stated. He was the best tuned to all those fashion disasters. Mrs Harrisons gave him a fierce look which put a quietus on Mr Harrisons laughter and made Aloise grin.

"Okay then shall I go to my room?"

"Ya sure. Wear your best."

She went inside. While going, she noticed that her parents took one copy of her book to the temple in their house and placed it in front of the Gods. It was a custom in the Hindus. Any new thing was first kept in front of the Gods to incur more blessings. She joined them a minute later after seeing.

It was 15 minutes to 5:30 and Aloise was in her best outfit. She was wearing a beautiful white one piece and light pearl jewellery. Her hair was of neck length and decently comb. It was 5:30 and Marie had arrived. Aloise was as usual was impressed by her beauty.

"You look great. I think you are the birthday girl." Aloise praised Marie.

"Thanks! But you are no less, Miss India."

Again an exaggeration."Thank you. Did you see what was getting cooked?"

"No, But I did smell it. It smelled awesome. "

"Well I hope so."

Aloise after getting ready came outside and her parents praised her for her lovely outfit.

It was 15 past 6 and her other 2 friends arrived.

"Wow man you surprised me. Your book is a masterpiece. Hello Uncle, Aunty. We met in AAI. I am Arpita."

"Hi I am Erika."

"Good to see you two here attending the function. You people make yourself comfortable and enjoy."

"A perfect reunion." said Marie.

They had a gala time. They discussed about Aloise's book, everybody's lifestyle and goals. It was a perpetual discussion which came to a halt when the food arrived. It was a perfect hotel style dinner. First, the starters then the main course, drinks and finally the dessert. It had to be so royal, after all it was a twin party. Here's the menu card designed by Mrs Harrisons which was shared in common with the 3.

The Desi Indiana.

1. **Starters**:- Masala Papad
2. **Drinks**
3. **Main Course**:-Amul Pav Bhajji
4. **Dessert**:- Surprise!!

   NOTE:- Dear customers, everything is unlimited and free of cost. Have a great time in our hotel.

How much she loved her mother and her ideas. Everyone was dying with hunger and was filled with excitement.

The first dish came. It was filled with onions, tomatoes, and was really picturesque. The taste was delicious. Then one by one the dishes came and they were simple awesome. The drink was a pineapple juice. The dessert which was a surprise element was a custard pudding filled with multilayer toping, cherries and a chocolate stick. Everyone was really surprised. It was by 7:30 that they felt satiated and thanked Aloise's mother for the delicious dinner.

It was time to leave. So everyone said Good night and went to their respective houses. It was only 3 of them left. Aloise, her mother and her father. Aloise was tired and so said Good night and went to her room. She changed and was ready to bed.

Everything till now was going as she had expected. She was in the awe of her book when she received an incoming call, it was Mr Ludin.

"Hallo sir. Aloise here."

"Hallo Aloise, I was a risky day indeed. I have already sent your money in cash through the post. I think you would get it by tomorrow or latest by the day after. Again, a very big Congratulation. It was your first book, which is a success. Have a good night and in future if you wish to publish any more books, please let me know. I wish you become a good writer; it is in your blood. One more important thing that you should know is that your book is sent in the foreign countries. In all probability, your book will gush through the foreign market in a year or so. "

"Thank you sir for all your help. It's great news. It's been pleasure working with you. Good Night."

This was no less than a cherry on the cake. It was a breath – taking day indeed......

Chapter 14

Americanoooo!!!

It was precisely 3 months before her Post Graduation programme would begin. She was on the American airport looking for her aunt. Her flight was an hour late. It was the first time ever that she had come to foreign. Her parents kept on insisting for their company but Aloise said that she wanted to go alone. She spoke to her aunt who lived in the US and she readily agreed to receive her.

"Hallo Aloise!", shouted her aunt. She wore a knee length red colour *kurta* which had a standing collar and black jeans. She was a good looking woman in her 40's. She always was a helping hand and an enthusiastic lady. She came and hugged Aloise.

"Hi aunty! Sorry for the inconvenience. ", Aloise apologized wholeheartedly.

"No apologies dear. We are meeting after such a long time. Congratulations for grabbing one of the finest MBA colleges across America."

"Thank you. I cannot resist telling you, how good you look. It seems you have lost lots of weight. Do you walk or go to gym? "

"*Suryanamaskars!* They are of great help. I have literally lost 5 kgs since then. But you look smart with your neck length hair. Come, let's get into a cab. I am hungry."

They walked to the taxi with the luggage and sat. It was a comfortable cab, thought Aloise. Much better than the taxi's of India.

"How's India, your mom and dad? Did you have any problem in the journey?"

"Well to be precise enough, India is in a state of morass. I think it has a very long way to go to elude corruption and poverty. India's economy is on an elusive ground. Coming back to my travel, no problem. It was luxurious. My parents are as merry as ever, and my mother has sent an *achaar* for you and some toys for my cousins. By the way, why didn't you get your children? Stella and Soji, right?"

"Ya right. Your memory is quite good. Were you eating a lot of almonds in India? They have their schools and will be back in 2 hrs."

"In which class they are?"

"Stella is now in 9th while Soji is in 5th. You stay in my house a couple of days until we find you a house."

"No thank you aunty. It's very kind of you, but I don't wish to cause any more inconveniences to you."

"Stop it. Don't be so formal. We will search a house for you together in the vicinity of your college. We could start that survey from today evening."

They reached her aunt's house which was very colossal from the inside. "Its really spacious. I like your house."

"Thank you dear."

They went inside and had something. Her aunt prepared pasta for both. Aloise was very hungry. She ate like a gourmand because her aunt was busy on the phone. Apparently she was talking to Aloise's parents, informing that she had safely landed to the US and that was eating pasta with the *achaar* which was very tasty. Later, Aloise spoke to them and she could hear a sigh of relief left on the other side and kept the phone. They just had their food when the door bell rang. Aloise opened it. It was Soji and Stella. They had grown big. It took more than a minute to recognize them. It was the same situation for the two siblings.

"Hi guys. Do you remember me?"

"If I am not mistaken, are you Aloise, my cousin from India?" it was Stella. She spoke English very fluently.

"Yes Stella. Meeting after a long time."

"Yes sis. My mom told me about you. Congrats for your Graduation."

The trio went inside. Aloise accompanied them for eating but this time as a spectator and not a player on field. After their lunch Aloise gave them their respective gifts. They were very happy seeing it.

It was 5 o clock, and the four of them were ready to go out for their survey. She was thrilled about staying in her own house all alone. They set off.

Chapter 15

The Survey

They first went to the place where her institution was located. It was a well furnished college. Aloise preferred going inside and so did others. They went inside and Aloise interacted with the staff there and she found them affable at her first interaction. She found out the necessary details and papers required on the first day.

Next big problem was to find her shelter, preferably nearby. They surveyed very circumspectly and shortlisted 5 of them. It was getting late, so they had their dinner outside in a hotel. They were bored and hence returned to the house. It was hectic day. The children went to bed immediately, leaving the two of them to talk.

"So, what have you thought about it? Which house do you think would be better? Any opinion? You have to make the decision."

"Well I think the nearer the better. I would like to go for the one near the Institution. Moreover, its rent is also affordable. What do you think?"

"A wise decision."

Aloise's phone was vibrating. It was her mother. She picked it energetically.

"Hello mother. How are you?

"Fine. What about you? What did you do today?"

“I am fine. I, aunty along with her 2 kids surveyed about houses on rent in this area. I have chosen one of them and we are going to go there tomorrow. I had a good lunch as well as dinner. For lunch I had pasta and dinner we had outside in a hotel.”

“Good. Is the location of the house good and safe? ”

“Ya mom. The best part of its location is that, it is near my allocated college.”

“Talk with your dad, beta.” She handed the phone to Mr Harrison’s.

“Hi dad, Whatsapp??”

“Living life king size. What about you?”

“Same here. Tomorrow I am going to finalise my house. Today my aunt has requested me to stay in hers.”

“Any issues with college or transport or anything?
Any assistance from our side?”

“No problem and no assistance of anything required Dad. Can I call you tomorrow morning? I am exhausted and feeling a bit sleepy. We came back just a few minutes ago.”

“Sure. Good night from both of us and All the best for tomorrow.”

“Thank you and Good night.”

Aloise switched off her phone after the call.

“My husband is on a tour to Germany and will be back in 4 days. So you can sleep with me in my room. Are you okay with that arrangement?”

"Perfect."

Aloise was really feeling the day's fatigue and wanted some rest. So she readily agreed and in no time they both were on the bed. She was going to have a big day ahead.

The following day was bright and vivid. They waved off the two children and then were going to go to the place they had decided the earlier day. Her aunt had taken a day off from her office. They straight away went to the lady in charge of the owner. They introduced themselves once again, this time formally and spoke to her to finalise the whole issue. The lady was a cheerful person. She was gracious and welcoming. They fixed the rent at 2000 per month and that she would start living just the next day onward.

"No miss. Aloise would start living here only a month later."

They signed the deal and came off.

"Aunty, I am comfortable to start right from tomorrow."

"I called my husband today morning. He said that it will take him more 4-5 weeks to disembark America. So till then I will be happy having your company in my house. What say?"

"Thank you aunty. It's really sweet of you to let me live with you guys. I will always be grateful to you guys. But---"

"No more courteousness."

They reached house and Aloise immediately called her mother to narrate her entire incident.

It was 3 in the afternoon when they reached home. Both of them were damn hungry. So they prepare noodles and added it with munchurian gravy. It was a mouth watering dish and both of them ate a great deal. They ate and ate until they could not have stuffed any more of it.

The two kids were back by 4. They had a book in their hands, one which was completely entrenched in my memory. Aloise had completely forgotten about it.

"Mom, look at this book. It is written by Aloise didi. I found it in the nearby stores so I just bought it."

"Aloise you wrote a book? You never told me about it."

"Actually aunty, I had forgotten that my book was going to hit the foreign stores by now. I published my book a day before the anniversary of my parents. It was a huge success in India but outside India I am a bit doubtful. Hope you like my book. Thanks Stella for getting a copy of it. "

"Oh Aloise I would definitely like to read it. Had you told me about it, I would have taken the first copy. But I would definitely read it."

In the following days the news fled about me as a budding writer. Everyone was appreciating Aloise, but she had not stuck her photo, so they did not know her as the writer.

One month went very swiftly and Aloise was shifting her things to the new house. She had already paid her first instalment. Her aunt was of great help. She helped Aloise in shifting many things. Within no time Aloise was settled. She spoke to her neighbours. Both of them were tolerable families. She reported her parents about it. They wished Aloise luck for her MBA program.

It was 1 month from now that her college was supposed to begin. She had to get the prescribed books for MBA. "Aunty, were will I find the books?"

"There is a shop besides your college which keeps all the books required for MBA. You want me to come with you to buy it for you? "

"No aunty. Thanks for all the support. Hereafter I can take it all alone."

"Okay then I will leave. Take care and if you need help of any kind please let me know, no hesitations please. You know my house, drop there at any point of time. I won't mind. And all the best for future."

"Thank you. Give my regards and love to the little ones."

Her aunt left. Aloise started to arrange her house properly. After that, she planned to go to the grocery store to get her some food and the books beside the college. She did not have a vehicle and so she had to go walking.

In the evening at around 5, she bought some bread, cheese and eggs which would be suffice her for a week. While her way back she picked up the books and was home by the night. She was so drained out that she kept everything in the fridge and took one or two bread with cheese for her dinner. Then she called her parents.

She explained them about her shifting and arrangement. She told them about the grocery and everything. It was by 9 that she was on the bed. It was the first time that she was going to sleep all alone on a foreign land. She was a bit scared but much more excited. For an hour or so she did not get sleep, so she said "*Hanuman Chalisa*" slowly in her mind and within next few minutes she fell asleep. She was eagerly waiting for the first day of her college.

Chapter 16

MBA – Here I Come!!

Aloise was on the footsteps of her new college of MBA. Her heart was really beating as fast as a cheetah. Courageously she went inside. She was wearing a black jeans and a knee length green colour kurta. As soon as she walked through the corridor people started looking at her. They were literally staring at her. She was feeling a bit over conscious.

But that's okay. She thought that it may be only because she is an Indian and had a very good fashion sense and so she gave an audacious walk through the corridor and reached her class.

To her horror the lecture had already started. Many questions were appearing in her head and she did not know what to do and so she merely knocked the door gently. The door unfastened and a fair man, most probably 35 years old came out with a dour look on his face.

"Come in late comer. Welcome. Now what is your excuse?"

"Well, the lecture was supposed to start at 9, right?" said Aloise. She checked her watch. To avoid delay she thought of reaching the school 20 minutes before, and now she was hearing that she was 40 minutes late. That was difficult for Aloise to digest. It did not go under her throat.

"Wrong. Any more questions?"

Clearing her throat she asked, "May I come in Professor?" That was the only question that she could ask to the professor. What questions she would ask the professor when she herself was in that parallel state.

“No. Anything else?”

Aloise wanted to tell him to stop being a martinet and start condoning her but she said, “Thank you sir. Can you please reconsider your decision? I am sorry for my delay. Henceforth I won’t make such a blunder, I promise.”

The Hitler seemed to be thinking for a long time. Then suddenly he saw his watch. He had realised that his lecture was about to get over.

“Come on, get in. Tomorrow sharp at 8.” He added, this time being a Stentorian,”8 in the morning, miss?”

“Aloise. Good morning.” The Hitler smiled at me for the first time in those 50 minutes.

Aloise realised that by this times all the 60 pair of eyes were on her. She was definitely in an imbroglio. She found herself an empty seat in the second last row and quickly sat on it and tried to avoid any eye contacts. The lecture continued, but her concentration was totally lost.

The lecture was over. There was no more a pin drop silence. The chattering started. Aloise was sure that it was about her and nothing else.

Suddenly she spotted a well-known face sitting 2 benches ahead of her. It was she, the juda, the Kleptomaniac. Even she saw Aloise. They made an eye contact after 15 complete years. She still had those innocent eyes. It was no less than a coincidence. She left her seat and advanced towards Aloise and extended her hand to present a gift. Aloise was taken aback.

Chapter 17

An Important Rendezvous

“What is this?”Aloise tried to sound as harsh as possible.

“A small remembrance. I know you did not wish to talk to me, but still I wanted to give you this from the past 15 years. You have probably misunderstood me completely. ” With this little piece of advice she went back to her place. Aloise found her eyes to be wet. She quietly seized it to avoid any more attention. She thought of opening it in her house. She somehow knew that Sofia was doing this for loaves and fishes. She did not want to keep any contacts with her.

Looking through the entire class, she could infer that 20% were Indians. She saw a girl working quite diligently on something. “Hi I am Aloise. What is your name?”

“I am Blossy. Are you from India?”

“Ya, and I think you are from America” She nodded. “Ummm. Can you tell me what that professor was teaching? ”

Blossy grinned, “He is teaching us Fundamentals of Statistics. Do you want me you explain it to you. I would be happy briefing you about it.”

“Sure.”

Blossy came to Aloise’s s bench and started to explain her. She explained it very eloquently and Aloise could clearly understand the entire lecture. “Thanks. I understood perspicuously. Are you mechanical engineer?”

“No an instrumental Engineer.”

“I have never heard of it.”

For another half an hour she briefed Aloise about Instrumental Engineering.”Interesting, isn’t it Aloise?”

“Very.”

The next lecture was about to begin. Aloise had got a new partner to work with. The new lecturer was a stout lady wearing full-size long spectacles. She seemed to be in her 40s. She introduced herself and her subject to the class quite glibly. Suddenly, Aloise noticed the benches of the classroom. She had not noticed it, as she was ill at ease in the earlier lecture.

She noticed that the benches were wooden and of 3 idiots style i.e. raised ones. She had always wanted to sit on those kinds of benches. Later in the evening, she called her parents and told them all the positive sides of the story. She sometimes did some cutting and pasting to form a new sentence as she did not want to recline profligately.

For example:-

“Mom, the professor smiled at me and asked me to come inside.”

“I met a new friend and an old friend of mine.”

“The benches were of Rancho style.”

……….

She spoke for 7-8 minutes and then ended it.

She looked around to see the mess in which her house was to be. It was 6 in the evening and she was going to clear the mess by 8. So she got every part of her body work rapidly. It was 7:30 and her work was almost done. By then she wasfamished with hunger. So she rushed to a nearby hotel and ordered for something. She had earned money by selling her 1st book. She had also heard from her parents that they had received the money of her book in India.

The next thing was to unwrap the gift given by Sofia. She opened it slowly. To her astonishment, she found that it contained her poems which she had given to her that time and the prize money Sofia had received. It also carried a letter, which read,

"Dear Aloise,

I know I have no rights of calling you "dear" but one last time. Don't treat me as your worst friend. I am aware of my mistakes and I know that I cannot undo them.

When I met you for the 1st time I never knew that we would be so good friends. But slowly as our friendship advanced I could see your immense creativity escalating. Even I wanted to have a poem of yours. I felt timid before you. So I planned to do it. I know my justifications are in vain but condone me for first and last time. I don't think that mistake should overlook our deep friendship. I had the most unforgettable moments of my life with you. I am sorry once again. I hope you will reconsider your decision. Our meeting again is not just a mere coincidence; it is something much more than that......

Plz tell me tomorrow.....About your final decision. I would be waiting in the 1st floor Girl's Common room. Lets me in lunch hour...

Also talking about your resent release, I loved your book as always. I was the first to buy the copy from stores.

Yours

Sofia."

Aloise read the letter two times just to understand Sofia's motives behind the letter. But she could not read her mind. She stopped stressing her minds and looked at the clock. It was perfect 9. She was already yawning hard. Moreover the following day, she was going to be on time, at 7:45. She was happy to see her poems back, safe in her hands. The prize money had delighted her even more. Ever since she had shifted to her new house she had never asked for even a penny from her parents. It was all the money that her book had given. And now this bonus was just titillating her. She was happy about her loyalty but still she could not neglect the act of theft.

She was dying to talk to her ever since she saw Sofia. Even she did not want to leave her friendship. It was her first one. Tomorrow she was going to confront Sofia and clear all the issues.

Chapter 18

Lost And Found

It was the 2nd day of her college and she was on time. But unfortunately, the first lecture was off. It was of the martinet's. She was sitting with Blossy, her new friend. Aloise grabbed the opportunity and went near Sofia and whispered in her ear. The next moment, both of them were facing each other in the common room.

"I am really sorry, Aloise. I know I made the biggest blunder of my life. But your animosity has tortured me even more. I can say you sorry a thousand times, but please don't leave me. Our friendship is much more precious. Please give me a chance." This time there was sense of truthfulness and contrition in her eyes that Aloise could sense without any pinch of doubt.

"I can give you a chance. But I cannot assure you about our superglue friendship which we once had.", said Aloise after thinking long.

"I am happy. Thank you." Sofia was indeed delighted. Both shaked hands and were back to their seats to attend the 2nd lecture. They were just in time.

"Hi frnds. Aftr a long tym.",

Aloise was chatting with her 3 friends. Only Marie was online. She had spoken to them for 3-4 months. She had just filled her net pack since her transfer.

"I am in America."

"Hi Aloise. Y dint u contact?"

"Busy arrngin tings. I am all alone in my new house. "

"Wooo.Gr8 feelin. Isn't it?"

"Indeed. Wat r u doin?"

"Finaly completed my course and a reputed fashion designer. To start off wit I am desinin for small models."

"Gr8. Congo.AL d bst for future."

"Ty. Same 2 u. Bye. In hurry."

"Ya."

Aloise waited for sometime but her other friends did not come online. Finally she typed.

"Erika, Arpita what about u guys??"

The following days were of goodwill. Sofia had changed by loads and masses. She was a totally a new human being. Their friendship deepened and she was again enjoying with her. They started eating together, sitting together and staying together. Apparently Sofia also was staying alone. Once when they were having their lunch in the canteen,

"Aloise when did you shift and where are you living?"

"I shifted 3 months before the college was about to begin. I live at 10 minutes of walking distance. What about you? "

"I live far from here. I give an amount of 3000to my land lords who are really cruel. I did not get any other place to stay."

There was a momentary silence.

"Aloise, if you don't mind can I stay with you? I promise I won't disturb you and would never interfere in your business."Aloise had expected this question. She thought for a minute or two. She did not want to take any decision in a hurry. They ate in complete silence.

"Okay. Let's live together. But we will never interfere in anyone's matters. I pay the house owner 2000 per month. We will divide it as 1000 per person per month. I have 1 room and a hall. May be you could take the hall for sleeping. Don't worry its big enough. And one more important thing that you should know, is that I don't have a television, I have a radio. If you are fine with this arrangement you shift tomorrow as I am going to pay her the 2nd instalment tomorrow. Deal?"

"Deal. I would join you from tomorrow. Today after college I will drop at your place. " Sofia immediately removed a note of 1000 from her pocket and gave it to Aloise.

Aloise still did not trust Sofia entirely but she was going to give her a chance. Moreover Aloise had not wanted to stay alone. So she took the note and they went inside the classroom for the next lecture. Aloise has never forgotten any of her good friends. She had not forgotten Blossy as well. Blossy had got a new friend totally. Well to be precise enough, Blossy had met the adonis of the college and was deeply interested in him. Blossy never told this to Aloise but Aloise was very good at understanding a person just by reading his or her facial expressions. They did not meet each other frequently but whenever they met they were in good humour.

The night before the shifting Aloise cleaned her entire house and made room for the new guest. She called Marie and her parents. Her parents were happy at Aloise's decision. Marie at first was shocked at such a coincidence and disapproved of her staying with Aloise. But then understanding Aloise and her condition she agreed. But she warned Aloise to stay away from Sofia.

Chapter 19

A BI – Union

“Wow, your house is much more spacious than mine. Thank you. Where should I keep my luggage? ”

“You could share my room for luggage. There is plenty of space. What should I make for you? Tea or coffee?”

“Let me help myself. I will sponsor the dinner. You relax.”

“Okay then let me show you the entire house, especially the kitchen.”

Their dinner was ready in 10 minutes. Sofia was good at cooking food. They had *parathas* for dinner.

“Where did you find *atta* in my kitchen?”Aloise was truly bewildered.

“I bought it from my place. How are the *parathas*? Do you like them?”

“Delicious. It is always been my favourite item. Thanks for such a feast.” Aloise was truly satisfied by her dinner for the first time in 4 months.

“Welcome. Happy to hear that it pleased you. Why don’t you write another book which will contain all your poems which you had written in 3rd or 4th standard.”

“I was chewing over that thought. May be it should wait for another 6 months or so.”

They went to bed at 9:30 pm sharp. They both went to college together and came back together. Days passed by at a very rapid pace and her one year of the MBA course was about to get over. In a blink of her eyes she got her MBA degree. She had everything walking in its place.

But what next??This question was of paramount importance. Sofia was going to do a job in America itself. Aloise pondered upon the job prospects in America seriously. She wanted to start her own industry. But should it wait??

Job?? Or an Entrepreneurship??

In America? Or In India?

Status :PERPLEXED.

Chapter 20

The Dream

The 7 decisions lead to only a single destination.

Just after Aloise's MBA, she got many job offers ranging right from 4lakhs to 20, 40 lakhs per year. Meanwhile, as suggested by Sofia, Aloise wrote one more book and the latter fetch her big prize. She had a remarkable career life and was always in contact with each of her friends. After around 10 years, she took courage to leave her job and start her own industry which was her dream plan. This was biggest gamble of her life. Till her 12th she had been cosseted severely and now she had to take a real big foot.

Her dream was to start her own mobile company, just as Samsung, Nokia etc. and decided to brand it as "IKON". She wanted to envelope the entire market by her "IKON mobiles". Interestingly, Aloise had done a course of mobile making, the circuits inside it and had a good knowledge of its designing and functioning. She did this course when she was doing her job. She mostly attended abroad jobs and always travelled back to India to visit her parents. Her first job gave her the first salary of her life. With this she bought her parents to abroad and put America under their nose. Not only America, after a few years she went to Germany. Wherever she went, she never forgot to take her parents and paraded them that picturesque place. She shared her idea of entrepreneurship with her parents who seemed to be thrilled by it and encouraged her.

Aloise thought of starting the industry in India itself, as the Indian government was giving good incentives and scope for female entrepreneurs. She deeply thought of it and started to shape the bricks. She was determined and her repeated failures that she had faced earlier had given her fortitude. Now she was on the limbo of her professional life.

Mr and Mrs Harrison lived in Pune and so Aloise was back in Pune to fire up the building blocks of "IKON". It took her 4 to 5 years to set the whole of her dream into motion. She hired people, mostly woman who had the tenacity to succeed. They made their first model named as "I LITHE". Aloise knew that as she had to compete with the chief brands, she had to give a star element in her "I LITHE". The following were its specifications.

The "I Lithe"

1. Highly Flexible. Easy to carry.
2. 6.5 inches when held taut and can be folded up to 3 times.
3. 13 mega pixels rear camera and 6 mega pixels front camera.
4. Built in GPS, ADVANCE DICTIONARY, 10 GAMES and MS OFFICE.
5. USB cord with FM radio.
6. Battery life :- 4000 mah
7. 2 GB RAM 16 GB hard disk and supports 4G connectivity.
8. Starting at just Rs.12,9999/-
9. 8mm thickness.
10. Android system: - Lollipop 5.1
11. Colours :- Black and White

Looking at the specifications anyone could have been baffled. But people did not respond to the mobile enthusiastically. Aloise could not understand why? She was in a welter and on asking her friends and conducting a small survey; she discovered that the second specification that she had so prominently framed had put many buyers in a dilemma. They were worried by the concept of folding a mobile. They thought what if by chance due to folding the functioning of mobile gets hampered? After all, the entire brand name was just coming in the market. How could someone take such a risk of spending 13000/-.

Aloise immediately amended the second specification and wrote in an urbane language.

2. 6.5 inches when held taut and convertible. 2 in 1. If folded once works as a mobile and if not, works as a note.

In a fraction of second the “I LITHE” mobiles flooded the markets of Pune. The reviews of the mobile were good and Aloise and her team were making progress. They received huge response after 4 – 5 months and Aloise gifted her parents that mobile. Her parents were over the moon and praised their daughter exultantly. Even her relatives and her friends bought the mobile and congratulated Aloise. The best part of the mobile was its name. Everyone was just crazy about the name. Their market grew substantially. “I LITHE ”was slowly getting approved by the market. Aloise was the happiest of all. It was her first grand success after the book.

Their “IKON” team continued to make new mobiles which could again capture the attentions of many. Sometimes they were not up their potentials and had to face a lot of criticism but life goes on and takes its own way.........

From The Writer's Desk

This virtually puts an end to Aloise's story. What she did later on is not of my concern because after this stage she is sure to have a bit of relaxation period as she has picked up her line of interest. But your story has just begun.

Hasn't it?????????

1. Criticism always comes free with Appreciation and success. It's just like appetizing *Vada-pav* in India with which green chilly is always complimentary. One must never grumble about it.
2. It is always noted that when bad luck comes, it portraits for decades while when good luck comes it is just like *gulab-jamuns* in front of famished person.
3. You must be a stoic. You must always heckle life and be a combatant and not a coward.
4. You must always do a SWOT (Strengths, Weakness, Opportunities and Threats) analysis.
5. Sometimes you may have to put your feet into the dirt around you only to come out of it unhurt and pristine. So always be optimistic towards whatever is happening. Always remember that Lotus which is the national flower of India grows in the dirt.
6. According to me there are various decisions that an individual can make, but there are 7 important decisions that are mandatory to be made.
7. I have just highlighted those 7 decisions.

My friends, let me again get this straight, the 7 most important decisions that one has to make in order to grow big strictly "**according to me**" are,

1. **A CHOICE OF FRIENDS**:-

   You normally become aware of the friend circle around you after your 8thstd. You are bound to receive many varieties during this period.

2. **CHOICE AFTER 10TH :-**

   This choice may not be that difficult for a person who is limpid about his strengths and weaknesses. For e.g. if a person likes maths and science, he must take Science stream, for someone whose arts is good should go for Fashion designing field etc.

3. **CHOICE AFTER 12TH :-**

   This is the most strenuous choice one has to make. It's not just innocent twelfth. It has *"12 different avatars"*.

i. New concept of Jr. College in Maharashtra. A rush for that.
ii. Sometimes a good college, with motley of virulent teachers.
iii. Being obsequious with the teachers for the internals, which is of great help in boards as well as in Engineering.
iv. Sometimes pandering to the needs of college for correction of lab journals.
v. Jr. College teachers are strict about attendance, timing and punctuality. But not strict about the English language, a tool with which they teach.

vi. Selection of coaching classes for competitive exams, which is become mandatory nowadays. It becomes difficult for a common man to select from a ruck of banal classes.

vii. **C**ompetition, **C**ompletion with no ground work **C**onstructions.

These days only solving papers are given a lot of value. Theory is just made sidetrack. In this world of competition no one is paying any attention to the Construction and Clearance of basic concepts.

viii. Learning IIT before learning its ABCD. Mostly the students get sandwiched here. As the JEE advances closer no time is given for theory clarifications.

ix. The brain work sometimes does not help. As a result some students go in depressions.

x. After getting the results, "Which is the most authentic college for Engineering or Doctor?" If engineering, then which branch?

xi. Stand for hours in the ARC's for brochure, receipt containing login id and password and document verification.

xii. Finally after all the hardships, everyone feels this,

"Are yaar, yeh sare acche college itne jaldi close kyun ho jateh hai. Thode aur rank par close hote toh shayad mujhe wahan admission mil jata."

4. CHOICE OF POST GRADUATION?:-

One usually stops after getting a degree, an official one. But one should never stop at this point.

5. CHOICE OF SETTLEMENT?? :-

This is yet another important choice that one has to make. One can study abroad or go to abroad after education or stay within country itself.

6. CHOICE OF HOSTEL ACCOMMODATION :-

You may find that choice number 5 and 6 are similar. But they are entirely different. Everyone wants a good college. For example, if a guy lives in Chinchwad and gets COEP, why won't he take it? He will either have to take the blatant buses or the halcyon hostels. Both have their own pros and cons.

i. Although hostels won't give you the fatigue which daily travelling gives, in hostels distractions and other activities like washing clothes, loitering etc. increases.

ii. On the other hand the up and down by buses will make you tired, but will not make you lethargic. You can eat the homemade food which is much healthier and tastier than the mess of hostels.

7. CHOICE OF TAKING RISK :-

This choice is the toughest and the most important of all. Everyone is fond of seeing James Bond. "Bond 007". Am I not right? Is it only because of the story which is terse with thrilling moments of incident and action? No. it is all about the new risks, the new tactics that he would use to cause mayhem to the villains. Isn't it?

It is true that if you never take a risk in your life no matter however meagre it is, you have never tried something new. All the people who are today, virtuosos

> of singing, dancing, composing etc. have at some time definitely taken risk. If you have an inborn talent don't waste time in thinking about, should I take a step forward, just do it. Follow your passion and you will never be in a fix. Rather the biggest risk in life is supposed to be following our own passions.

There one path on which everyone has to walk, someday or the other,

> Now I am really in the wilds, cutting the tortuous path through the tangled jungles, wading knee deep through noisome swamps, breathing the steaming pernicious air, fetid with moribund and decadent undergrowth. My native guides are getting refractory and I was trying to hold them in hand, first with cajolery and adulation. I still had not learned the tricks of the trade.

My friends, many more situations of this kind will occur which may seem in intractable and insuperable but one thing that I can surely assure you is that it won't be an impasse.

You will always be surrounded by censorious people but you must always pay less attention to them and always imbibe what is of use and chuck out what is useless. If you start a task complete it pretentiously. You must always have the alacrity of winning.

Hard work never goes waste. Guys, you must trust me on this. If you do hard work may be no one could guarantee you your expected results. But if you do hard work and not get the results you would at least be in a position to face the people around you and tell them that I had done my part. Now if you don't do hard work and not get results, you will definitely fall on your face. That is the core difference between them.

Expecting results without even doing hard work is foolishness.

Moreover remember one very important thing,

Unleash Your Fear,
Face The Bitter,
Enjoy The Meagre,

Have A Mammoth Heart,
Always Condone Those Who Ask,
Be A Mask Of Surprises,
Pray For No More Quizzes Of Crisis.

Follow the 7 decisions and reach your destination

****

www.ingramcontent.com/pod-product-compliance
Ingram Content Group UK Ltd.
Pitfield, Milton Keynes, MK11 3LW, UK
UKHW040030200726
13854UKWH00001B/454